??

THE
JUNIOR QUESTION COLLECTION

MORE THAN 300 QUESTIONS ABOUT

BOOKS

SPORTS

PEOPLE & PLACES

MATH
25
+ 32
57

SCIENCE

AND MORE

Written by Linda Schwartz • Illustrated by Beverly Armstrong

??

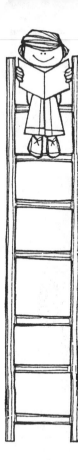

The Learning Works

Edited by Sherri M. Butterfield

Dedicated to Bob and Vicki with love.

The purchase of this book entitles the individual teacher to reproduce copies for use in the classroom.

The reproduction of any part for an entire school or school system or for commercial use is strictly prohibited.

No form of this work may be reproduced or transmitted or recorded without written permission from the publisher.

Copyright © 1988
THE LEARNING WORKS, INC.
P. O. Box 6187
Santa Barbara, CA 93160
All rights reserved.
Printed in the United States of America.

Introduction

This book is a collection of more than three hundred questions covering such topics as geography, government, grammar, history, literature, mathematics, music, presidents, science, and sports. It is intended for use in the classroom, at home, or anywhere children have empty minutes to fill, and should be ideal on rainy days, before recess, during parties, or while traveling.

The questions have been placed two to a page. Questions on any one page cover different topics but are of a similar degree of difficulty. The pages have been arranged within the book so that the questions progress from easy through medium to hard. In general, questions on the first fifty pages should be easier to answer than questions on the last fifty pages.

3

57,875

The Junior Question Collection
© 1988–The Learning Works, Inc.

No collection of questions would be complete without a collection of answers. In this book, the collection of answers appears at the back of the book, on pages 166-184. To make needed answers easier to find, they have been listed by page number and keyed by letter to a particular position on the page. Thus, answer **a** is for the question on the left side of the page, and answer **b** is for the question on the right side of the page. (See diagram.)

a	b

A Special Message to Teachers

The ways to use this book in your classroom are almost endless. To begin with, of course, you can open it to any page and ask a few questions to fill those last minutes before lunch or recess.

Or you can turn the questions into a **self-checking game**. Select pages on which the questions are appropriate for the grade level you teach. Duplicate some of these pages and cut the questions apart. Glue each question to one side of a plain 4-inch-by-6-inch index card. Glue or write the corresponding answer on the other side of the card. Laminate the cards and make them available as part of a classroom display or learning center.

5

The Junior Question Collection
© 1988–The Learning Works, Inc.

You can turn the process of answering the questions into a **research activity**. Select pages on which the questions are somewhat challenging for the grade level you teach. Duplicate these pages and make cards as above, but do not write the answers on the cards. Instead, write the appropriate page number and answer letter. Distribute the cards and challenge individual students or teams to find and record the answers within some specified time limit. Then, check their results against the answer key. You may want to keep score on a chart or graph by the week or month.

You can use the questions on a particular topic as part of a **classroom display** on that topic. For example, look through the book and select a group of questions about U.S. presidents. Duplicate the pages on which they appear. Cut out the questions you have selected and post them on a classroom bulletin board or wall. Make blank cards available and suggest that students write and illustrate additional questions on the same topic, and add them to the display.

In addition, you can use these questions for question bees, for staged classroom quiz shows that follow a radio or television format, as motivators for students who get bored with routine classwork, and as pleasant bonus activities for students who have completed their assignments and are looking for something more to do.

In short, you may find that The Junior Question Collection provides a lot of answers for a busy teacher in a bustling classroom.

A Special Message to Parents

The ways to use this book are almost endless. To begin with, of course, it's perfect for filling indoor time on rainy days, amusing a child who is ill, or making the miles go faster when you travel. For example, your child might use it to stage a **quiz show** in radio or television format. For a change, let him be the quizmaster while you play contestant and try to supply the answers.

Use selected questions as a **party game**. Choose teams, ask questions, keep score, and reward the winners with prizes of some kind. Use this book to **sharpen research skills**. If your child does not know an answer, instead of telling him, help him look it up in a dictionary, encyclopedia, or other similar reference book. Or use this book as the inspiration for an **art activity**. Supply plain 4-inch-by-6-inch index cards and a black felt-tipped marking pen, and suggest that your child add to The Junior Question Collection.

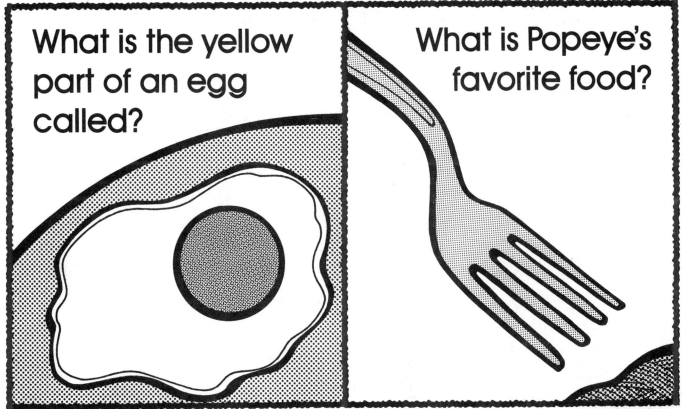

What is the yellow part of an egg called?

What is Popeye's favorite food?

9

The Junior Question Collection
© 1988–The Learning Works, Inc.

What is the tallest animal in the world?

How many days are in a week?

What two colors
are mixed
to make pink?

Which insects
make honey?

11

The Junior Question Collection
© 1988–The Learning Works, Inc.

Name Donald Duck's three nephews.

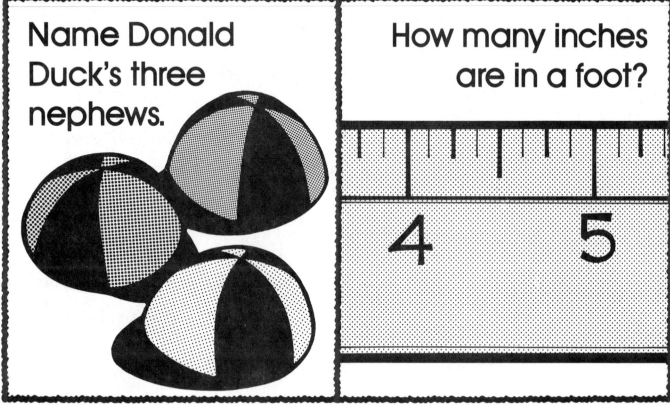

How many inches are in a foot?

In the United States, Thanksgiving comes during which month?

What coin is worth twenty-five cents?

13

How many wheels does a tricycle have?

What is another name for a baby frog?

my mother and her mother

me↓

How is your mother's mother related to you?

How many months are in a year?

15

What two colors
are mixed
to make green?

French fries
are made from
what vegetable?

To what family do tigers and lions belong?

Land ho!

Which Italian explorer discovered America in 1492?

The Junior Question Collection
© 1988–The Learning Works, Inc.

Name Charlie Brown's pet beagle.

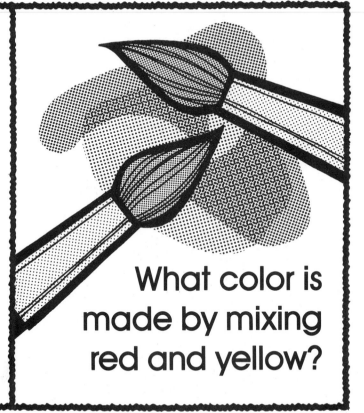

What color is made by mixing red and yellow?

In Roman numerals, for what does the letter V stand?

In which month do we celebrate Valentine's Day?

The Junior Question Collection
© 1988–The Learning Works, Inc.

What name is given to that part of your body where your hand joins your arm?

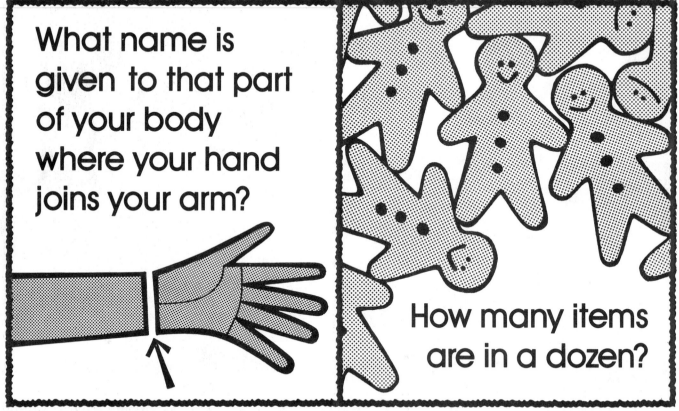

How many items are in a dozen?

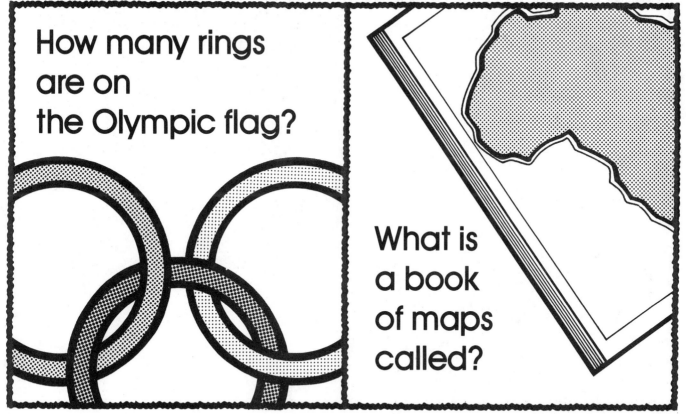

How many rings
are on
the Olympic flag?

What is
a book
of maps
called?

21

What is
the name of
Christopher Robin's
teddy bear?

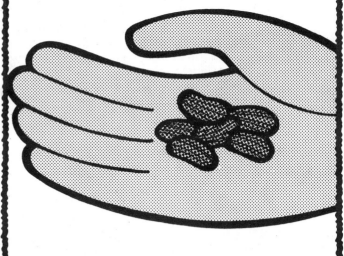

What are
dried grapes
called?

Is okra
a vegetable,
a bird, or a fish?

How many innings
are in
a baseball game?

23

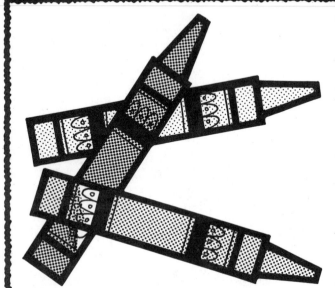

Name the three primary colors.

What do you call a place where living wild animals are housed and displayed?

What is
a baby sheep
called?

What do you call
the day on which
a person was
born?

MARCH

1

2

Dr. Seuss
born
1904

25

What large country lies directly north of the United States?

What is the name of Mickey Mouse's dog?

In Roman numerals, for what does the letter X stand?

How many stripes are on the American flag?

27

What is cheese made from?

What is a baby goat called?

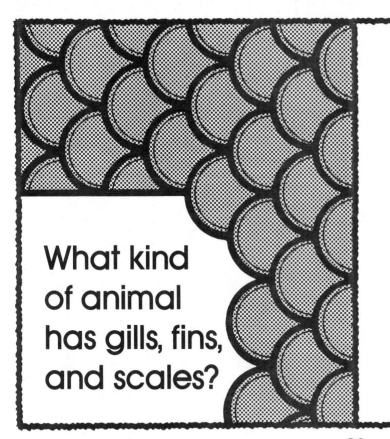

What kind
of animal
has gills, fins,
and scales?

How many quarts
are in a gallon?

ROCKY ROAD·R

POLAR POWER
ICE CREAM
ONE HALF GALLON

29

The Junior Question Collection
© 1988–The Learning Works, Inc.

Name the elephant that could fly.

What closed shape has three sides?

123

With which sport do you connect the words <u>pigskin</u>, <u>punt</u>, and <u>safety</u>?

PUNT!

What is a baby cat called?

On which holiday are you supposed to wear something green?

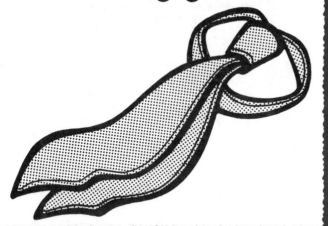

Which organ pumps blood to all parts of the human body?

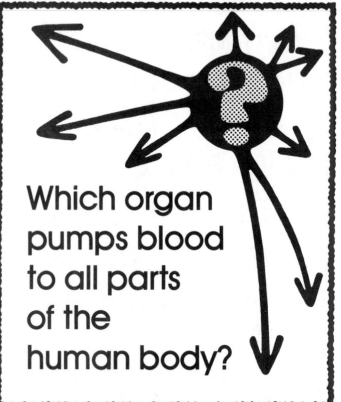

What do you call a salted cracker baked in the shape of a knot?

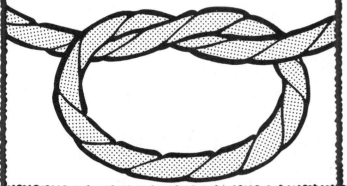

What is a baby cow called?

The Junior Question Collection
© 1988–The Learning Works, Inc.

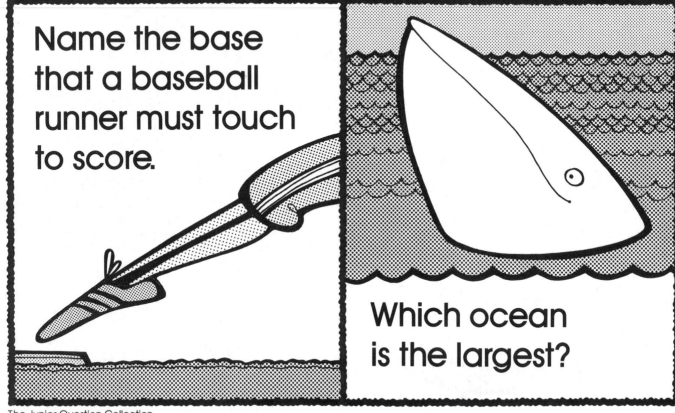

Name the base that a baseball runner must touch to score.

Which ocean is the largest?

What time is it when the little hand of a clock is between six and seven and the big hand is on six?

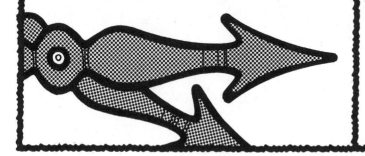

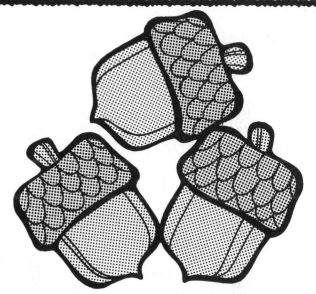

What kind of tree produces acorns?

The Junior Question Collection
© 1988–The Learning Works, Inc.

What kind
of animals were
Walt Disney's
Chip 'n' Dale?

How many feet
are in a yard?

What horselike
animal has
dark and light
stripes on its body?

Whose picture
is on the
one-dollar bill?

The Junior Question Collection
© 1988–The Learning Works, Inc.

What do the stars on the American flag represent?

What do we call a flash of light caused by electricity passing from one cloud to another?

The result obtained when two or more numbers are added together is called what?

What is the outer covering of a tree called?

The Junior Question Collection
© 1988–The Learning Works, Inc.

In Where the Wild Things Are, what is the name of the boy?

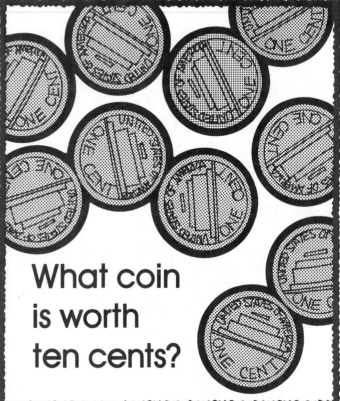

What coin is worth ten cents?

Which sport has a championship game known as the Super Bowl?

Which ocean is the smallest?

To burn, what gas must a fire have?

What do you call a ship that can travel under water?

Which planet is called the red planet?

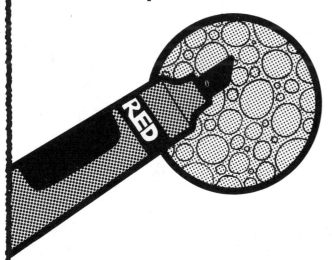

How many sides does a die have?

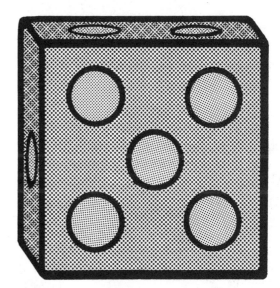

In which direction does the sun rise?

What are the names of the two major political parties in the United States?

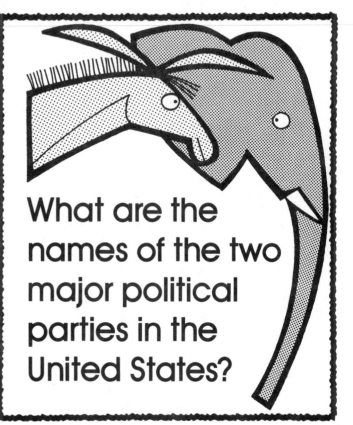

What country did
Christopher
Columbus
hope to find?

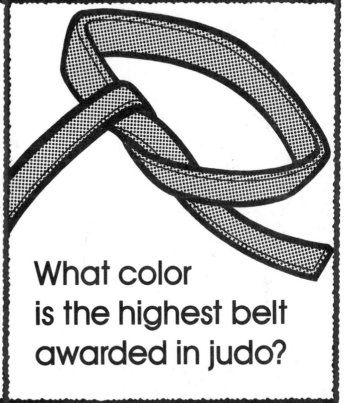

What color
is the highest belt
awarded in judo?

The Junior Question Collection
© 1988–The Learning Works, Inc.

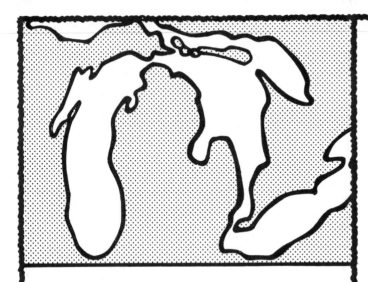

How many lakes make up the Great Lakes?

Name the instrument most commonly used by a doctor to listen to your heart.

Which baglike organs in your chest enable you to breathe?

What holiday is celebrated on the Fourth of July?

The Junior Question Collection
© 1988–The Learning Works, Inc.

What do you call the padded, leather-covered seat used by the rider of an animal?

Name the planet on which we live.

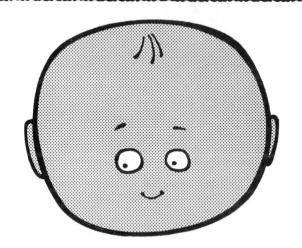

If someone has twins, how many babies are born?

How many arms does a starfish have?

49

The Junior Question Collection
© 1988–The Learning Works, Inc.

What time is it when the little hand of a clock is between three and four and the big hand is on six?

Which star is the source of the earth's light and heat?

How many points are given for a goal in soccer?

On what ship did the pilgrims sail to America?

The Junior Question Collection
© 1988–The Learning Works, Inc.

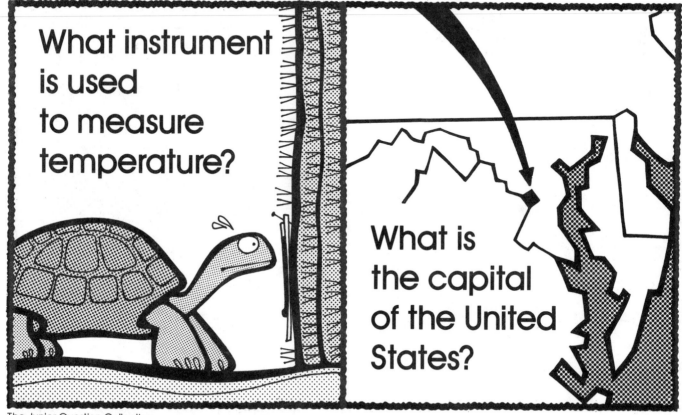

What instrument is used to measure temperature?

What is the capital of the United States?

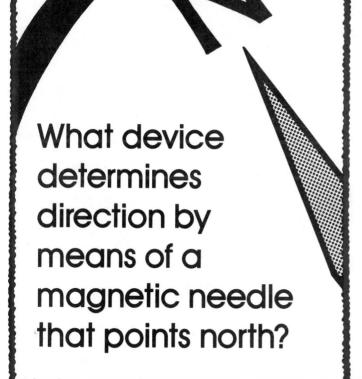

What device determines direction by means of a magnetic needle that points north?

In which harbor would you find the Statue of Liberty?

53

The Junior Question Collection
© 1988–The Learning Works, Inc.

How many players are on a boys' basketball team?

What color is on the top of a traffic signal?

What is
a long, snakelike
fish called?

How many ounces
are in a pound?

Where do paper and wood come from?

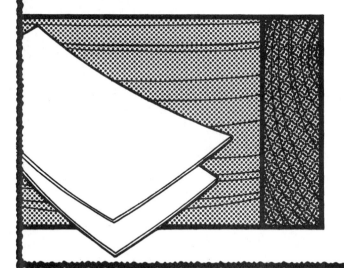

Who was the first president of the United States?

What device is used to weigh things?

27 28

Which month has only twenty-eight days?

In what city is the Golden Gate Bridge?

Name the hot liquid that flows from volcanoes.

In what month is Mother's Day celebrated?

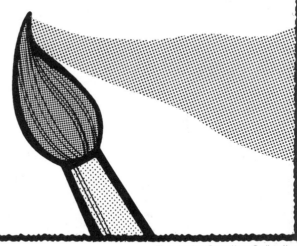

Is scarlet a shade of red, yellow, or blue?

The Junior Question Collection
© 1988–The Learning Works, Inc.

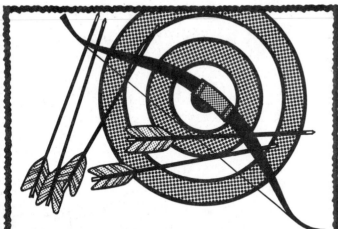

Name the sport in which bows and arrows are used.

What kind of factory did Willy Wonka have?

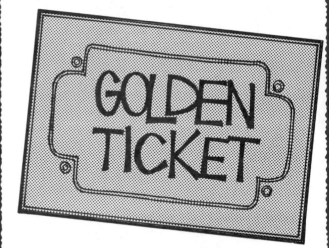

How many people sing in a trio?

What do you call a group of fish?

The Junior Question Collection
© 1988–The Learning Works, Inc.

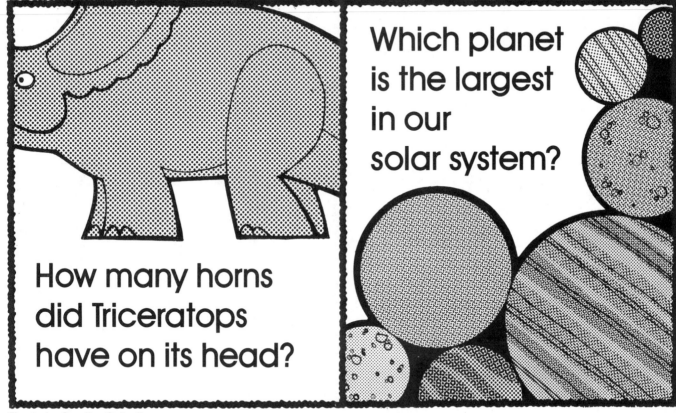

How many horns did Triceratops have on its head?

Which planet is the largest in our solar system?

How many letters are in the alphabet?

A rectangle has how many sides?

The Junior Question Collection
© 1988–The Learning Works, Inc.

How many points does a team get for a field goal in football?

Is a heron a vegetable, a reptile, or a bird?

In what state is
Walt Disney World?

How many legs
does a spider
have?

ALL RIGHT! A SPARE!

What sport are you playing if you get a spare?

How many days are in a year?

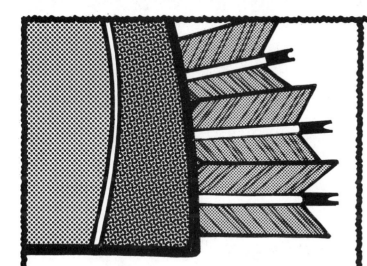

What do you call
a case
for holding arrows?

Which part of
speech tells how,
when, or where
about a verb,
adjective, or an
adverb?

The snail moved slowly.

67

The Junior Question Collection
© 1988–The Learning Works, Inc.

In which month does winter officially begin?

How old must a person be to vote in national elections in the United States?

What name is given to the remains of plants and animals preserved in rocks?

How many weeks are in a year?

The Junior Question Collection
© 1988–The Learning Works, Inc.

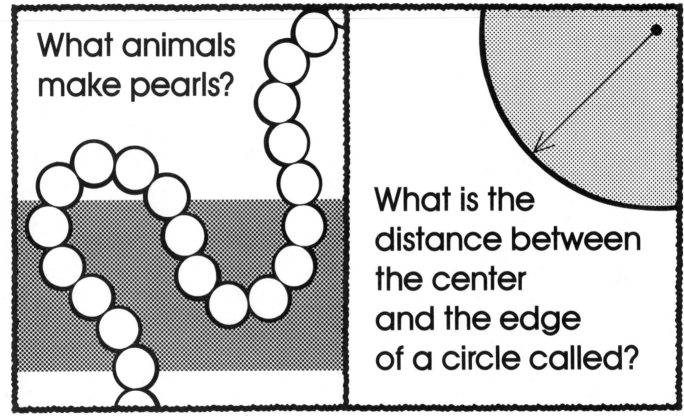

What animals make pearls?

What is the distance between the center and the edge of a circle called?

How many years are in a decade?

With what organs do most fishes breathe?

Who was the first American astronaut to orbit the earth in a spacecraft?

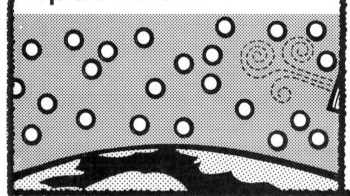

For what do the letters FBI stand?

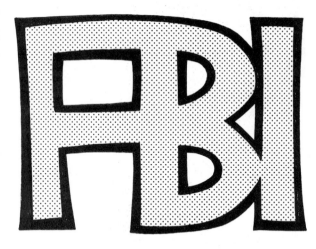

Ah!

The words <u>ah</u>, <u>oh</u>, and <u>wow</u> are examples of which part of speech?

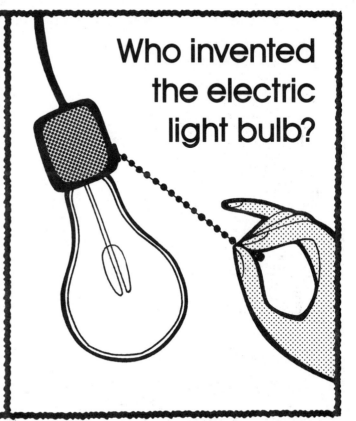

Who invented the electric light bulb?

The Junior Question Collection
© 1988–The Learning Works, Inc.

What do we call a number that expresses one or more equal parts of a whole?

How many permanent teeth do humans have?

What is the name
of a tube
and mouthpiece
used by swimmers
to breathe
underwater?

Which is
the largest state
in the
United States?

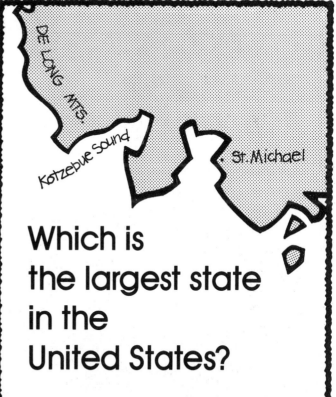

DE LONG MTS.

Kotzebue Sound

St. Michael

75

In which country were the first Olympic Games held?

What name is given to a tropical cyclone that occurs in the Pacific Ocean?

In what popular board game would you find a pawn?

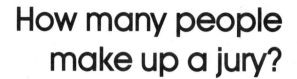

How many people make up a jury?

The Junior Question Collection
© 1988–The Learning Works, Inc.

What part
of a plant
soaks up water
from the soil?

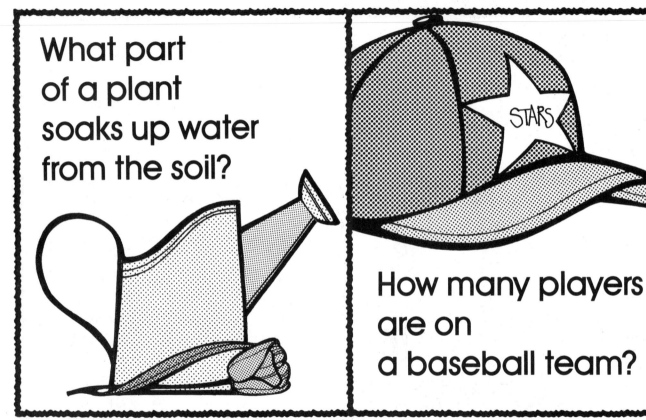

How many players
are on
a baseball team?

5-2=3

The number from which another number is subtracted is called what?

What do you call a dried plum?

The Junior Question Collection
© 1988–The Learning Works, Inc.

With which sport do you associate the terms Australian crawl, butterfly, and treading?

How many pounds are in a ton?

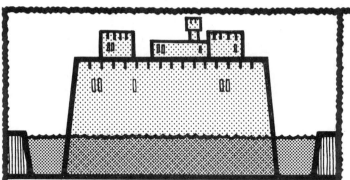

What do we call a deep ditch that surrounds a castle and is filled with water?

What color is khaki?

ENAMEL PAINT

KHAKI

The Junior Question Collection
© 1988–The Learning Works, Inc.

In which state would you find the Alamo?

In Roman numerals, for what does the letter L stand?

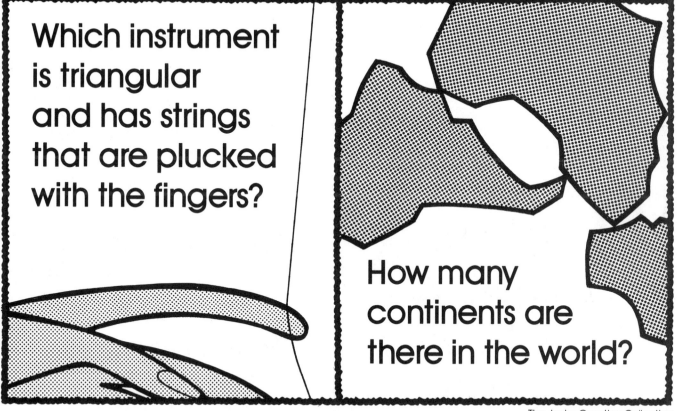

Which instrument is triangular and has strings that are plucked with the fingers?

How many continents are there in the world?

The Junior Question Collection
© 1988–The Learning Works, Inc.

What bird is the national symbol of the United States?

How many years are in a century?

What is
the black part
of your eye
called?

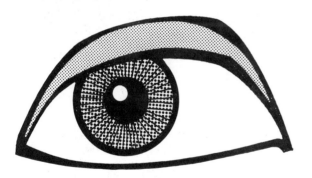

**tickle toss
tap trudge
think type
tug twinge**

Which part
of speech
shows action or
a state of being?

The Junior Question Collection
© 1988–The Learning Works, Inc.

What holiday is celebrated on the last Monday in May?

Historically, a pirate robbed what?

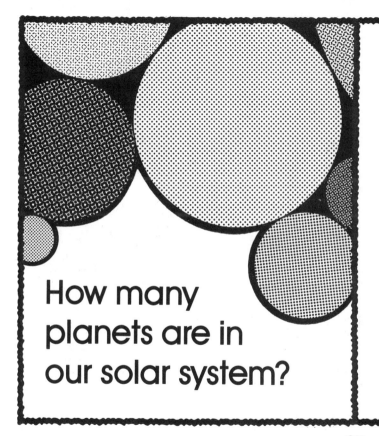

How many planets are in our solar system?

In which state is the city of Detroit?

What is
a closed figure
with five sides
called?

GOU-LASH?

What is
another name
for goulash?

Which Spanish explorer discovered Florida while looking for the fountain of youth?

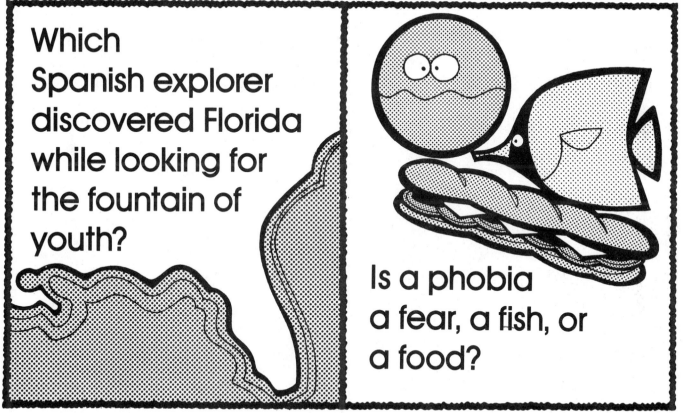

Is a phobia a fear, a fish, or a food?

The Junior Question Collection
© 1988–The Learning Works, Inc.

Name the soft, deerskin shoes made and worn by American Indians.

From what animal does beef come?

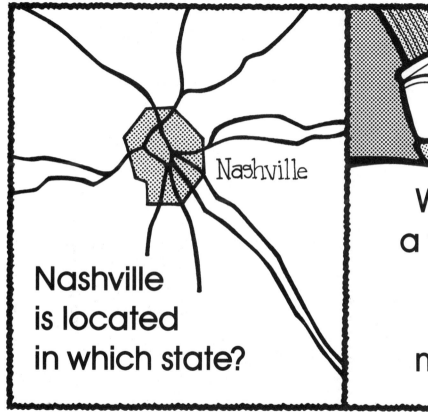

Nashville
is located
in which state?

What do we call
a footrace run on
a course
measuring 26
miles 385 yards?

What is a baby kangaroo called?

In a fraction, what is the number below the line called?

Which country in Europe is shaped like a boot?

How many players are on a football team?

The Junior Question Collection
© 1988–The Learning Works, Inc.

Name the U.S. war in which the North fought against the South.

What animal is called "the ship of the desert"?

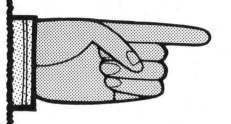

$$\frac{3}{4}$$

In a fraction, what is the number above the line called?

Of what material are glaciers made?

The result obtained when two or more numbers are multiplied is called what?

2 × 3 = 6 ↓

Would you find fleece on a sheep, a snake, or a spider?

Name the plant that has thick stems covered with spines and is found in hot, dry places.

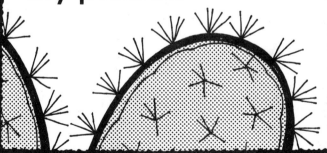

Who invented the telephone?

Which part of speech tells which one, what kind, or how many about a noun or pronoun?

A stop sign has how many sides?

What do you call a group of elephants?

What is the largest national park in the United States?

Who is the author of <u>Tales of a Fourth Grade Nothing</u>?

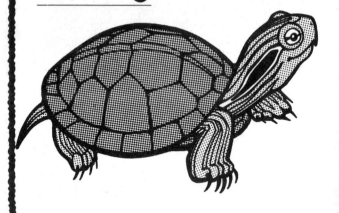

How many cups are in a pint?

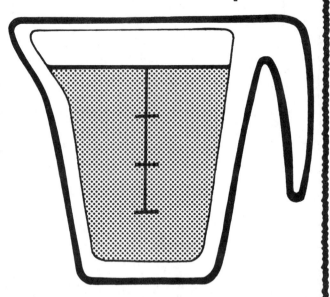

In what board game do you "crown," or "king," a playing piece?

King me!

In what building does the president of the United States live?

What is
a marionette?

Chocolate is made
from the bean
of what plant?

In which state is the Empire State Building?

How many legs does an insect have?

The Junior Question Collection
© 1988–The Learning Works, Inc.

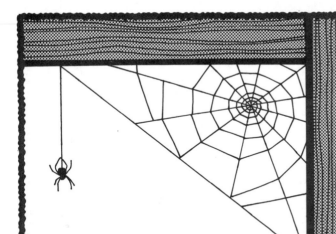

In the book Charlotte's Web, what was the name of the pig?

Whose picture is on the five-dollar bill?

Who was the first black baseball player in the major leagues?

How many sections are in an orchestra?

The Junior Question Collection
© 1988–The Learning Works, Inc.

Are penguins found in the Arctic or the Antarctic?

What is sleet?

MCM

In Roman numerals, for what does the letter C stand?

Is an aster a fish, a flower, or a food?

The Junior Question Collection
© 1988–The Learning Works, Inc.

Who wrote Dear Mr. Henshaw and Ramona the Pest?

In which direction does the sun set?

In which sport would you hear the term full-court press?

In which state would you now find the London Bridge?

fifteen-love!

In which sport would you hear the words <u>ace</u>, <u>love</u>, and <u>set</u>?

Which country borders the United States on the south?

Was Pablo Picasso most famous as an artist, an author, or a poet?

Which famous canal links the Atlantic and Pacific oceans?

111

The Junior Question Collection
© 1988–The Learning Works, Inc.

Which American swimmer won seven gold medals in the 1972 Olympics?

A sphinx has the body of what animal?

Is a gnu
a bird, a fish,
or a mammal?

How many sisters
were in the book
Little Women?

What is the name of the one-legged captain in Moby Dick?

In which state is Mount Rushmore?

Name the imaginary circle around the earth that is the same distance from the North Pole and the South Pole.

What is another name for Indian corn?

The Junior Question Collection
© 1988–The Learning Works, Inc.

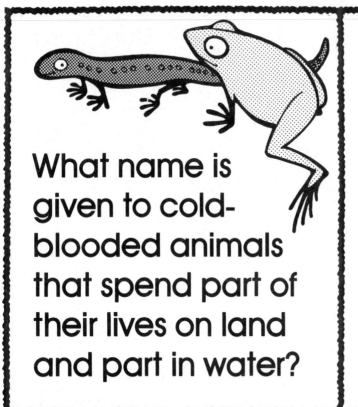

What name is given to cold-blooded animals that spend part of their lives on land and part in water?

Egypt is located on which continent?

How many justices sit on the U.S. Supreme Court?

What was the name of Dorothy's dog in the movie The Wizard of Oz?

The Junior Question Collection
© 1988–The Learning Works, Inc.

The Japanese art of paper folding is called what?

BRAZIL

On which continent would you find the country of Brazil?

How is the child of your aunt or uncle related to you?

What do you call a group of bees?

The Junior Question Collection
© 1988–The Learning Works, Inc.

I have a dream...

Who began
a famous speech
with the words,
"I have a dream"?

What do we call
a person
who studies
plants?

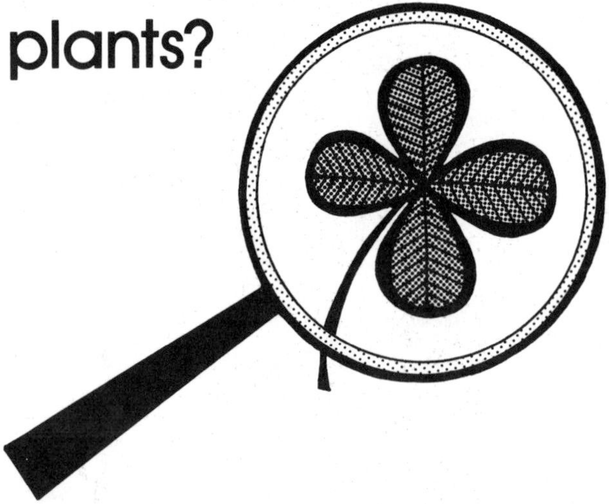

What do we call people who leave one country to make their home in another country?

Who wrote the book Charlotte's Web?

The Junior Question Collection
© 1988–The Learning Works, Inc.

What was the name of Paul Bunyan's blue ox?

Name the American Indian princess who helped Captain John Smith.

What do you call the five lines and the four spaces between them on which musical notes are written?

In which country would you find the Great Wall?

Name the artist
who painted
the Mona Lisa.

The Gold Rush
of 1849
brought people
to which state?

Who wrote "The Ugly Duckling" and "The Emperor's New Clothes"?

How many bones are found in the adult human body?

125

Where does rubber come from?

Who wrote The Adventures of Tom Sawyer?

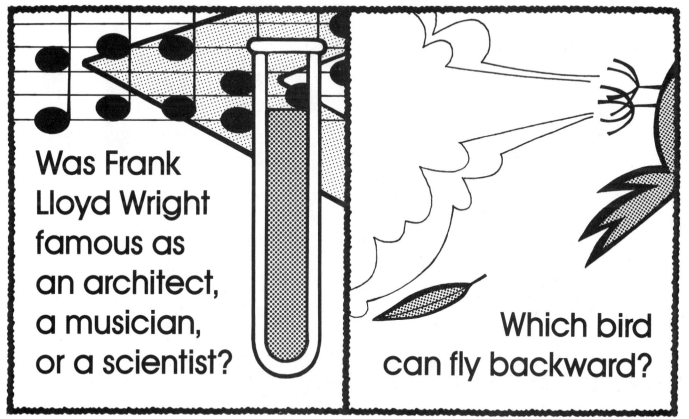

Was Frank Lloyd Wright famous as an architect, a musician, or a scientist?

Which bird can fly backward?

The Junior Question Collection
© 1988–The Learning Works, Inc.

What instrument locates and measures the intensity of earthquakes?

What body of water is the saltiest and the lowest in the world?

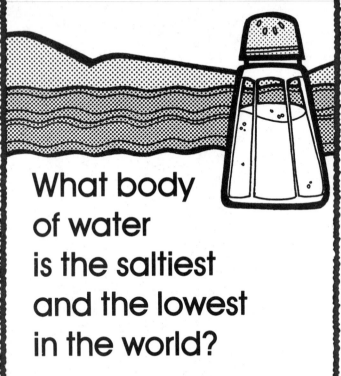

Who invented the lightning rod?

Is Johann Strauss famous for composing marches or waltzes?

What name is given to the sign on a musical scale that tells the pitch for each line and space?

What do we call a plant that lives only one year?

The Junior Question Collection
© 1988–The Learning Works, Inc.

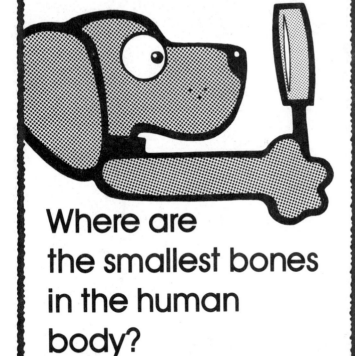

Where are
the smallest bones
in the human
body?

In which state
is the
Liberty Bell?

What queen of Spain helped Christopher Columbus?

How many legs does a lobster have?

Who wrote "The Star Spangled Banner"?

China is located on which continent?

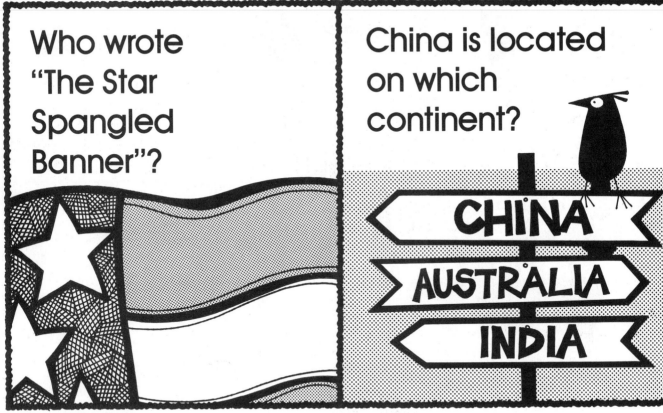

What kind of tree is the largest in the world?

What do you call a group of lions?

Who is known as the "Father of the Constitution"?

Where did the Wizard of Oz live?

How many years is one term of office for a U.S. president?

How many squares are on a checkerboard?

The Junior Question Collection
© 1988–The Learning Works, Inc.

What do we call a change in the U.S. Constitution?

Which dinosaur has a name that means "thunder lizard"?

Which state is known as the Grand Canyon state?

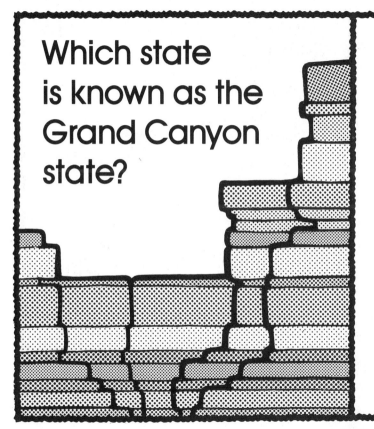

In Roman numerals, for what does the letter M stand?

The Junior Question Collection
© 1988–The Learning Works, Inc.

How many keys does a piano have?

What is a male pig called?

Which snake
is the longest
in the world?

42, 43, 44,
45, 46, 47,
48, 49, 50.

Name the last
state admitted
to the Union.

Which U.S. president lived at Mount Vernon?

How many zeros are in one million?

What do we call someone who rides a horse in a race?

What is the longest river in the world?

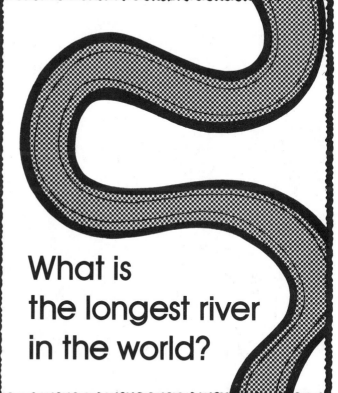

The Junior Question Collection
© 1988–The Learning Works, Inc.

What do the letters VCR stand for?

On which continent are the Andes Mountains?

About how long does the moon take to make one trip around the earth?

What is the name of the trophy awarded to the year's best movie?

The Junior Question Collection
© 1988–The Learning Works, Inc.

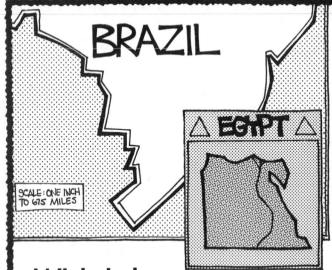

BRAZIL

SCALE: ONE INCH
TO 675 MILES

EGYPT

Which is
farther north,
Brazil or Egypt?

What is
a female horse
called?

On a poison ivy plant, how many leaves are in each cluster?

James Naismith is said to have originated what popular sport?

The Junior Question Collection
© 1988–The Learning Works, Inc.

According to legend, who was the leader of the Knights of the Round Table?

What plants must pandas have to survive?

In Roman
numerals,
for what does
the letter D stand?

The ruler
of England
lives in what
famous palace?

How many points does a football team receive for a safety?

Who was the first president to live in the White House?

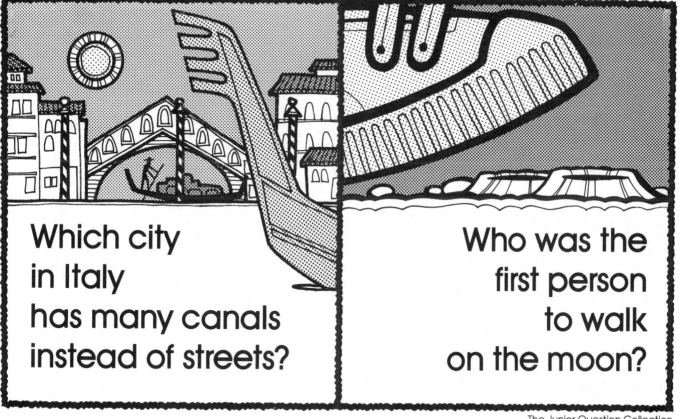

Which city
in Italy
has many canals
instead of streets?

Who was the
first person
to walk
on the moon?

The Junior Question Collection
© 1988–The Learning Works, Inc.

How many people make up the president's cabinet?

What building is the tallest in the world?

Who was
the first woman
appointed to the
U.S. Supreme
Court?

What was
Babe Ruth's
real name?

The Junior Question Collection
© 1988–The Learning Works, Inc.

Who was the first woman to cross the Atlantic Ocean in an airplane?

What is the colored part of the human eye called?

Who became president after Richard Nixon resigned?

In which sport is the most important tournament called the World Cup?

How many body parts does an insect have?

Who invented the telegraph?

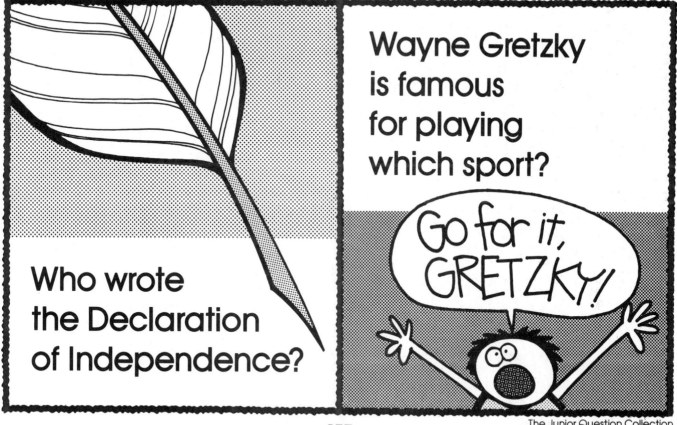

What is another name for an animal doctor?

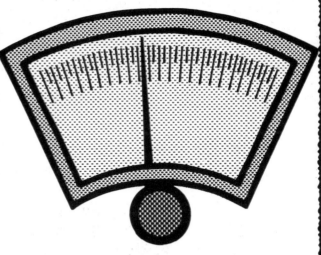

What instrument is used to detect radioactivity?

What name is given to the branched horns on a male deer's head?

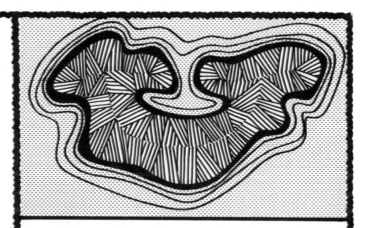

What is the name for a body of land that is surrounded by water?

The Junior Question Collection
© 1988–The Learning Works, Inc.

On which continent is the Sahara Desert?

With which sport do you associate Dick Button, Peggy Fleming, and Dorothy Hamill?

A duet
is played
by how many
musicians?

For what game
is Bobby Fisher
famous?

What is the capital of France?

Are salamanders reptiles or amphibians?

Which planet is the smallest in our solar system?

What is the highest court in the United States?

Who was president of the United States during most of the Civil War?

What breed of dog is the smallest?

On the Fahrenheit scale, at what temperature does water boil?

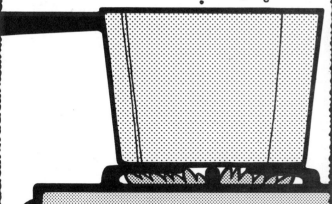

Is John Philip Sousa famous for composing marches or waltzes?

Page 9
a. the yolk
b. spinach

Page 10
a. a giraffe
b. seven days

Page 11
a. white and red
b. bees

Page 12
a. Huey, Dewey, and Louie
b. twelve inches

Page 13
a. November
b. a quarter

Page 14
a. three wheels
b. a tadpole or polliwog

Page 15
a. She is your grandmother.
b. twelve months

Page 16
a. yellow and blue
b. potatoes

Page 17
a. the cat family
b. Christopher Columbus

Page 18
a. Snoopy
b. orange

Page 19
a. five
b. February

Page 20
a. the wrist
b. twelve items

Page 21
a. five rings
b. an atlas

Page 22
a. Winnie-the-Pooh
b. raisins

Page 23
a. a vegetable
b. nine innings

Page 24
a. red, yellow, and blue
b. a zoo

The Junior Question Collection
© 1988–The Learning Works, Inc.

Page 25
a. a lamb
b. a birthday or birth date

Page 26
a. Canada
b. Pluto

Page 27
a. ten
b. thirteen stripes

Page 28
a. milk
b. a kid

Page 29
a. a fish
b. four quarts

Page 30
a. Dumbo
b. a triangle

Page 31
a. football
b. a kitten

Page 32
a. Saint Patrick's Day
b. the heart

Page 33
a. a pretzel
b. a calf

Page 34
a. home plate
b. the Pacific Ocean

Page 35
a. 6:30
b. an oak tree

Page 36
a. chipmunks
b. three feet

Page 37
a. the zebra
b. George Washington's

Page 38
a. the fifty states
b. lightning

Page 39
a. the sum
b. bark

Page 40
a. Max
b. a dime

The Junior Question Collection
© 1988–The Learning Works, Inc.

Page 41
a. football
b. the Arctic Ocean

Page 42
a. oxygen
b. a submarine

Page 43
a. Mars
b. six sides

Page 44
a. in the east
b. the Democratic Party
   and the Republican Party

Page 45
a. India
b. black

Page 46
a. five lakes
b. a stethoscope

Page 47
a. your lungs
b. U.S. Independence Day

Page 48
a. a saddle
b. Earth

Page 49
a. two babies
b. five arms

Page 50
a. 3:30
b. the sun

Page 51
a. one point
b. the <u>Mayflower</u>

Page 52
a. a thermometer
b. Washington, D.C.

Page 53
a. a compass
b. New York Harbor

Page 54
a. five players
b. red

Page 55
a. an eel
b. sixteen ounces

Page 56
a. trees
b. George Washington

Page 57
a. a balance or scale
b. February

Page 58
a. San Francisco
b. lava

Page 59
a. May
b. red

Page 60
a. archery
b. a chocolate factory

Page 61
a. three people
b. a school

Page 62
a. three horns
b. Jupiter

Page 63
a. twenty-six letters
b. four sides

Page 64
a. three points
b. a bird

Page 65
a. Florida
b. eight legs

Page 66
a. bowling
b. 365 or 366 days

Page 67
a. a quiver
b. the adverb

Page 68
a. December
b. eighteen years old

Page 69
a. fossils
b. fifty-two weeks

Page 70
a. oysters
b. the radius

Page 71
a. ten years
b. gills

Page 72
a. John Glenn
b. Federal Bureau of Investigation

Page 73
a. the interjection
b. Thomas Alva Edison

Page 74
a. a fraction
b. thirty-two teeth

Page 75
a. snorkel
b. Alaska

Page 76
a. Greece
b. typhoon

Page 77
a. chess
b. twelve people

Page 78
a. the roots
b. nine players

Page 79
a. the minuend
b. a prune

Page 80
a. swimming
b. 2,000 pounds

Page 81
a. a moat
b. brown or tan

Page 82
a. Texas
b. fifty

Page 83
a. a harp
b. seven continents

Page 84
a. the bald eagle
b. one hundred years

Page 85
a. the pupil
b. the verb

Page 86
a. Memorial Day
b. ships at sea

Page 87
a. nine planets
b. Michigan

Page 88
a. a pentagon
b. beef stew

Page 89
a. Ponce de León
b. a fear

Page 90
a. moccasins
b. cattle (cow, steer, etc.)

Page 91
a. Tennessee
b. a marathon

Page 92
a. a joey
b. the denominator

Page 93
a. Italy
b. eleven players

Page 94
a. the Civil War
b. a camel

Page 95
a. the numerator
b. ice

Page 96
a. the product
b. a sheep

Page 97
a. cactus
b. Alexander Graham Bell

Page 98
a. the adjective
b. eight sides

Page 99
a. a herd
b. Yellowstone National Park

Page 100
a. Judy Blume
b. two cups

Page 101
a. checkers
b. the White House

Page 102
a. a puppet
b. the cacao plant

Page 103
a. New York
b. six legs

Page 104
a. Wilbur
b. Abraham Lincoln

Page 105
a. John Roosevelt ("Jackie") Robinson
b. four sections

Page 106
a. in the Antarctic
b. Sleet is frozen rain.

Page 107
a. one hundred
b. a flower

Page 108
a. Beverly Cleary
b. in the west

Page 109
a. Arizona
b. basketball

Page 110
a. tennis
b. Mexico

Page 111
a. an artist
b. the Panama Canal

Page 112
a. Mark Spitz
b. a lion

Page 113
a. a mammal
b. four sisters

Page 114
a. Captain Ahab
b. South Dakota

Page 115
a. the equator
b. maize

Page 116
a. amphibians
b. Africa

Page 117
a. nine justices
b. Toto

Page 118
a. origami
b. South America

Page 119
a. He or she is your cousin.
b. a swarm

Page 120
a. Martin Luther King, Jr.
b. a botanist

Page 121
a. emigrants
b. E.B. White

Page 122
a. Babe
b. Pocahontas

Page 123
a. a staff
b. in China

Page 124
a. Leonardo da Vinci
b. California

Page 125
a. Hans Christian Andersen
b. 206 bones

Page 126
a. a tree
b. Mark Twain or Samuel Clemens

Page 127
a. an architect
b. the hummingbird

Page 128
a. a seismograph
b. the Dead Sea

Page 129
a. Benjamin Franklin
b. waltzes

Page 130
a. George Washington's
b. a cheetah

Page 131
a. a clef
b. an annual

Page 132
a. in the ear
b. Pennsylvania

Page 133
a. Queen Isabella
b. ten legs

Page 134
a. Francis Scott Key
b. Asia

Page 135
a. a sequoia
b. a pride

Page 136
a. James Madison
b. in the Emerald City of Oz

Page 137
a. four years
b. sixty-four squares

Page 138
a. an amendment
b. Brontosaurus

Page 139
a. Arizona
b. one thousand

Page 140
a. eighty-eight keys
b. a boar

Page 141
a. the reticulated python
b. Hawaii

Page 142
a. George Washington
b. six zeros

Page 143
a. a jockey
b. the Nile River

Page 144
a. a video cassette recorder
b. South America

Page 145
a. approximately 28 days or one month
b. the Oscar

Page 146
a. Egypt
b. a mare or filly

Page 147
a. three leaves
b. basketball

Page 148
a. King Arthur
b. bamboo plants

Page 149
a. five hundred
b. Buckingham Palace

Page 150
a. two points
b. John Adams

Page 151
a. Venice
b. Neil Armstrong

Page 152
a. fourteen
b. the Sears Tower in Chicago, Illinois

Page 153
a. Sandra Day O'Connor
b. George Herman Ruth

Page 154
a. Amelia Earhart
b. the iris

Page 155
a. Gerald Ford
b. soccer

Page 156
a. three body parts
b. Samuel F.B. Morse

Page 157
a. Thomas Jefferson
b. ice hockey

Page 158
a. a veterinarian
b. a Geiger counter

Page 159
a. antlers
b. an island

Page 160
a. Africa
b. figure skating

Page 161
a. two musicians
b. chess

Page 162
a. Paris
b. amphibians

Page 163
a. Pluto
b. the Supreme Court

Page 164
a. Abraham Lincoln
b. the chihuahua

Page 165
a. 212 degrees
b. marches

THE LEARNING WORKS

LW 279

ISBN 0-88160-169-1